A COLLECTION OF POETRY

BY

ROBERT E. HOWARD

British Library Cataloguing-in-Publication Data
A catalogue record for this book is available from the
British Library

Contents

Robert E. Howard. 1

Adventure. 3

Adventurer 3

The Alamo 5

Always Comes Evening. 5

Ambition 7

An American 8

An American Epic. 9

At The Bazaar 10

Aw Come On And Fight! 11

Babel. 12

But The Hills Were Ancient Then 13

The Choir Girl. 14

Crete. 14

Dead Man's Hate. 15

Deeps 18

Dreamer. 18

Dreaming On Downs. 19

Dreams Of Nineveh 20

Easter Island 21

Empire's Destiny 21

Eternity. 23

Fables For Little Folk 24

Feach Air Muir Lionadhi Gealach Buidhe Mar Or 25

Flaming Marble. 26

Forbidden Magic. 27

The Gates of Nineveh 28

Girl 29

A Great Man Speaks 29

The Harp of Alfred 30

Illusion. 31

Ivory in the Night 32

Jack Dempsey 33

John L. Sullivan. 34

Kid Lavigne is Dead 36

The Kissing of Sal Snooboo 37

A Lady's Chamber. 38

Laughter. 39

Lesbia 39

Libertine 42

Life 43

Lines to G. B. Shaw 44

Lust 45

The Maiden of Kercheezer 45

Miser's Gold 46

Monarchs 47

Moon Mockery 48

The Moor Ghost 48

The Mountains of California 49

Nun 50

Ocean-Thoughts 50

The One Black Stain 51

One Blood Strain 55

One Who Comes at Eventide 57

Poet 58

Private Magrath of the A.E.F 58

Prude 60

Rebellion 60

Red Thunder 61

Repentance 62

The Riders of Babylon 64

The Ride of Falume. 65

The Robes of the Righteous. 67

A Roman Lady 69

Romance 70

Roundelay Of The Roughneck 72

Rules of Etiquette 75

Sailor. 77

The Sands of Time 77

The Sea. 78

Secrets. 80

Serpent. 82

Shadow of Dreams 83

Skulls and Dust. 85

The Skull in the Clouds 86

Solomon Kane's Homecoming 90

A Song of Cheer 94

The Song of the Bats. 95

Sonora to Del Rio 96

Surrender 97

Tarantella 100

The Tempter. 102

Tides 104

To a Woman. 105

To the Contended 106

Toper 107

A Tribute to the Sportsmanship of the Fans. 107

Visions 108

The Voices Waken Memory 109

The Weakling. 110

A sappe ther wos and that a crumbe manne... 111

After the trumps are sounded... 111

Against the blood red moon a tower stands... 112

All the crowd... 112

And Dempsey climbed into the ring and the crowd... 113

Hills of the North! Lavender hills... 114

Match a toad with a far-winged hawk... 114

Mingle my dust with the burning brand.... 117

Moonlight and shadows barred the land... 117

Old Faro Bill was a man of might... 118

Rebel souls from the falling dark... 119

Scarlet and gold are the stars tonight... 119

Swords glimmered up the pass... 120

The spiders of weariness come on me... 123

There were three lads who went their destined ways... 124

There's an isle far away on the breast of the sea... 126

We are the duckers of crosses... 128

Robert E. Howard

Robert Ervin Howard was born in Peaster, Texas in 1906. During his youth, his family moved between a variety of Texan boomtowns, and Howard – a bookish and somewhat introverted child – was steeped in the violent myths and legends of the Old South. Although he loved reading and learning, Howard developed a distinctly Texan, hardboiled outlook on the world. He became a passionate fan of boxing, taking it up at an amateur level, and from the age of nine began to write adventure tales of semi-historical bloodshed. In 1919, when Howard was thirteen, his family moved to the Central Texas hamlet of Cross Plains, where he would stay for the rest of his life.

At fifteen Howard began to read the pulp magazines of the day, and to write more seriously. The December 1922 issue of his high school newspaper featured two of his stories, 'Golden Hope Christmas' and 'West is West'. In 1924 he sold his first piece – a short caveman tale titled 'Spear and Fang' – for $16 to the not-yet-famous Weird Tales magazine. He published with the magazine regularly over the next few years. 1929 was a breakout year for Howard, in that the 23-year-old writer began to sell to other magazines, such as Ghost Stories and Argosy, both of whom had previously sent him hundreds of rejection slips. In 1930, he began a correspondence with weird fiction master H. P. Lovecraft which ran up to his death six years later, and is regarded as one of the great correspondence cycles in all of fantasy literature.

It was partly due to Lovecraft's encouragement that Howard created his most famous character, Conan the Cimmerian. Conan – a barbarian-turned-King during the Hyborian Age, a mythical period of some 12,000 years ago – featured in seventeen Weird Tales stories between 1933 and 1936, and is now regarded as having spawned the 'sword and sorcery' genre, making Howard's influence on fantasy literature comparable to that of J. R. R. Tolkien's. The Conan stories have since been adapted many times, most famously in the series of films starring Arnold Schwarzenegger.

Howard was enjoying an all-time high in sales by the beginning of 1936, but he was also deeply upset by the ill health of his mother, who had fallen into a coma. On the morning of June 11, 1936, he asked an attending nurse whether she would ever recover, and the nurse replied negatively. Howard walked to his car, parked outside the family home in Cross Plains, and shot himself. He died eight hours later, aged just thirty.

Adventure

I am the spur
That rides men's souls,
The glittering lure
That leads around the world

Adventurer

Dusk on the sea; the fading twilight shifts'
The night wind bears the ocean's whisper dim—
Wind, on your bosom many a phantom drifts—
A silver star climbs up the blue world rim.
Wind, make the green leaves dance above me here
And idly swing my silken hammock—so;
Now, on that glimmering molten silver mere
Send the long ripples wavering to and fro.
And let your moon-white tresses touch my face
And let me know your slim-armed, cool embrace
While to my dreamy soul you whisper low.

Dream—aye, I've dreamed since last night left her
tower
And now again she comes on star-soled feet.
Welcome, old friend; here in this rose-gemmed bower

I've drowsed away your Sultan's golden heat.
Here in my hammock, Time I've dreamed away
For I have but to stretch a hand out, lo,
I'm treading langurous shores of Yesterday,
Moon-silvered deserts or the star-weird snow;
I float o'er seas where ships are purple shells,
I hear the tinkle of the camel bells
That waft down Cairo's streets when dawn winds
blow.

South Seas! I watch when dusky twilight comes
Making vague gods of ancient, sea-set trees.
The world path beckons—loud the mystic drums—
Here at my hand the magic golden keys
That fit the doors of Romance, Wonder, strange
Dim gossamer adventures; seas and stars.
Why, I have roamed the far Moon Mountain range
When sunset minted gold in shimmering bars.
All eager eyed I've sailed from ports of Spain
And watched the flashing topaz of the Main
When dawn was flinging witch fire on the spars.

I am content in dreams to roam my fill
The vagrant, drifting sport of wind and tide,
Slave of the greater freedom, venture's thrill;
Here every magic ship on which I ride.

Gold, green, blue, red, a priceless treasure trove,
More wealth than ever pirate dared to dream.
My hammock swings—about the world I rove.
The sunset's dusk, the dawning's glide and gleam,
Moon-dappled leaves are murmuring in the wind
Which whispers tales. Lo, Tyre is just behind,
Through seas of dawn I sail, Romance abeam.

The Alamo

For days they ringed us with the flame
For days their swarming soldiers came
The battle wrack was gory
We perished in the smoke and flame,
To give the world their traitor shame
And our undying glory

Always Comes Evening

Riding down the road at evening with the stars or
steed and shoon
I have heard an old man singing underneath a copper
moon;
"God, who gemmed with topaz twilights, opal portals

of the day,

"On our amaranthine mountains, why make human souls of clay?

"For I rode the moon-mare's horses in the glory of my youth,

"Wrestled with the hills at sunset-- till I met brass-tinctured Truth.

"Till I saw the temples topple, till I saw the idols reel,

"Till my brain had turned to iron, and my heart had turned to steel.

"Satan, Satan, brother Satan, fill my soul with frozen fire;

"Feed with hearts of rose-white women ashes of my dead desire.

"For my road runs out in thistles and my dreams have turned to dust.

"And my pinions fade and falter to the raven wings of rust.

"Truth has smitten me with arrows and her hand is in my hair--

"Youth, she hides in yonder mountains -- go and see her, if you dare!

"Work your magic, brother Satan, fill my brain with fiery spells.

"Satan, Satan, brother Satan, have known your fiercest Hells."

Riding down the road at evening when the wind was
on the sea,
I have heard an old man singing, and he sang most
drearily
Strange to hear, when dark lakes shimmer to the
wailing of the loon,
Amethystine Homer singing under evening's copper
moon.

Ambition

Build me a gibbet against the sky,
Solid and strong and long miles high,
Let me hang where the high winds blow
That never stoop to the world below,
And the great clouds lumber by.
Let the people who toil below
See me swaying to and fro,
See me swinging the aeons through,
A dancing dot in the distant blue.

An American

Sing of my ancestors!
　Sing of them with pride!
Sing of fair America,
　Green prairies and blue tide!
One was born in County Cork!
　Hail the shamrock green!
(One was named Abraham
　Simeon Levine.)
One held rule in Dundee,
　Friend of the Montrose.
(One sold nuts and apples
　Where the river Tiber flows.)
One drank ale in Devonshire,
　One scaled Lomond's crags.
(One grew up in Warsaw
　And peddled clothes and rags.)
One sailed out from Liverpool,
　Bold and free and glad.
(One lended cash at high
　Rates in Petrograd.)
Och, oi, oi, and hoot mon!
　Gott sie dank go bragh!
Gevald! Be dommed! Diavoli!
　America iss braw!

Shure, its meself thot loves the land,
    Vy shouldn't I? Oi oi!
Some fellow he no lika diss,
    I'm nae you kind o' boy!
Its aiche mon for his ain, py hell!
    A feller got to stand
An' tella people who he iss
    And brag on his own land!
Vun nation unt vun langvitche!
    Oi! And go for business fine
To Michael Israel Malcolmsky
    Gammettio O'Stein.

An American Epic

The autumn sun was gettin' low, the day was mighty windy,
When Hiram shot the hired man that kissed his girl Dorindy.
Them two was in the orchard there,
    for apples birds was peckin'
When old man Hiram hove in view
    and busted up their neckin'.
The hired man he took it out across the fields and ditches

But Hiram drawed a perfect bead
   and shot him in the breeches.
The hired man he flagged it on, for he knew other
ladies—
But Robert Frost can write the rest, or he can go to
Hades.

At The Bazaar

There breaks in the bazaar of Zanzibar,
   red surge of life on life;
At eve there came through the sunset's flame
   a man with a dripping knife.
"Eunuchs a score and seven more
   I've made today," said he,
"The blood and tears of all my years
   I've caused would fill a sea.
"Search far, search far from Zanzibar
   for youths of many lands
"For my hungry steel and the glee I feel
   when they writhe beneath my hand
He laid him down where the stains lay brown
   on the floor of the gelding room,
And his gory blade as it down was laid
   clanged like a tone of doom.

By Robert E. Howard

In sleep he leered and clawed his beard
  with fingers black with gore;
The ghosts of dead men came from Hell
  and staked him to the floor.

Aw Come On And Fight!

On my hands and knees in a scarlet pool
I heard the referee toll,
And the crowd roared: "Kill the yellow bum!"
Like the sea along a shoal.

I sprang, I struck, I crushed his skull
With a sudden desperate swing,
He died with his eyes to the glaring lights
And his back to the canvassed ring.

The referee counted above the dead,
I swayed and clung to the ropes,
And the crowd roared: "Yellow! Both of em's bums!"
Like the seas on the beaches slopes.

Babel

Now in the gloom the pulsing drums repeat,
   And all the night is filled with evil sound;
I hear the throbbing on inhuman feet
   On marble stairs that silence locks around.

I see black temples loom against the night,
   With tentacles like serpents writhed afar,
And waving in a dusky dragon light
   Great moths whose wings unholy tapers char.
Red memory on memory, tier on tier,
   Builds up a tower, time and space to span;
Through world on world I rise, and sphere on sphere,
To star-shot gulfs of lunacy and fear—
   Black screaming ages never dreamed by man.

Was this your plan, foul spawn of cosmic mire,
To freeze my soul to stone and icy fire,
To carve me in the moon that all mankind
May know its race is futile, weak and blind—
A horror-blasted statue in the sky,
   That does not live and nevermore can die?

By Robert E. Howard

But The Hills Were Ancient Then

Now is a summer come out of the sea,
　And the hills that were bare are green.
They shower the petals and the bee
　On the valleys that laze between.

So it was in the dreaming past,
　And life is a shifting maze,
Summer on summer fading fast,
　In a mist of yesterdays.

Out of the East, the tang of smoke,
　The flight of the startled deer,
A ringing axe the silence broke,
　The tread of the pioneer.

Saxon eyes in a weathered face,
　Cabins where trees had been,
Hard on the heels of a fading race,
　But the hills were ancient then.

Up from the South a haze of dust,
　The pack mules' steady pace,
Armor tarnished and red with rust,
　Stern eyes in a sun-bronzed face.

The mesquite mocked the flag of Spain,
   That the wind flung out again,
The grass bent under the pack mule train—
   But the hills were ancient then.

The Choir Girl

I have a saintly voice, the people say;
   With Elder Blank I send the music winging—
   I smile and compliment him on his singing—
By God, I'd rather hear a jackass bray.
   I nod and smile to all the pious sisters—
   I wish their rears were stung with seven blisters.
That youthful minister, so straight and slim—
I'd trade my soul for one long night with him.

Crete

The green waves wash above us
Who slumber in the bay
As washed the tide of ages
That swept our race away.

Our cities - dusty ruins;
Our galleys - deep sea slime;
Our very ghosts, forgotten,
Bow to the sweep of Time.

Our land lies stark before it
As we to alien spears,
But, ah, the love we bore it
Outlasts the crawling years.

Ah, jeweled spires at even -
The lute's soft golden sigh -
The Lion-Gates of Knossos
When dawn was in the sky.

Dead Man's Hate

They hanged John Farrel in the dawn amid the marketplace;
At dusk came Adam Brand to him and spat upon his face.
"Ho neighbors all," spake Adam Brand, "see ye John Farrel's fate!
"Tis proven here a hempen noose is stronger than man's hate!

15

For heard ye not John Farrel's vow to be avenged upon
me
Come life or death? See how he hangs high on the
gallows tree!"
Yet never a word the people spoke, in fear and wild
surprise-
For the grisly corpse raised up its head and stared with
sightless eyes,

And with strange motions, slow and stiff, pointed at
Adam Brand
And clambered down the gibbet tree, the noose within
its hand.
With gaping mouth stood Adam Brand like a statue
carved of stone,
Till the dead man laid a clammy hand hard on his
shoulder bone.

Then Adam shrieked like a soul in hell; the red blood
left his face
And he reeled away in a drunken run through the
screaming market place;
And close behind, the dead man came with a face like
a mummy's mask,
And the dead joints cracked and the stiff legs creaked

with their unwonted task.

Men fled before the flying twain or shrank with bated
breath,
And they saw on the face of Adam Brand the seal set
there by death.
He reeled on buckling legs that failed, yet on and on
he fled;
So through the shuddering market-place, the dying
fled the dead.

At the riverside fell Adam Brand with a scream that
rent the skies;
Across him fell John Farrel's corpse, nor ever the twain
did rise.
There was no wound on Adam Brand but his brow
was cold and damp,
For the fear of death had blown out his life as a witch
blows out a lamp.

His lips were writhed in a horrid grin like a fiend's on
Satan's coals,
And the men that looked on his face that day, his stare
still haunts their souls.
Such was the fate of Adam Brand, a strange, unearthly
fate;

For stronger than death or hempen noose are the fires
of a dead man's hate.

Deeps

There is a cavern in the deep
  Beyond the sea-winds brawl;
Where the hills of the sea slope high and steep,
And dragons sleep
And serpents creep
There is a cavern in the deep
  Where strange sea-creatures crawl.

Dreamer

I live in a world apart
  A world that has no link with this drab earth.
A vague, melodious world, where breezes start
  Soft joys and gay-hued mirth.

By Robert E. Howard

Dreaming On Downs

I marched with Alfred when he thundered forth
To break the crimson standards of the Dane;
I saw the galleys looming in the north
And heard the oar-locks and the sword's refrain.

And far across the pleasant Wessex downs
The chanting of the spearmen broke the lyre,
Till where the black thorn forest grimly frowns
We sang a song of doom and steel and fire.

Death rode his pale horse through the dreaming sky
All through that long red summer afternoon,
And night and silence fell, when silently
The dead men lay beneath a cold white moon.

Now Alfred sleeps with all the swords of yore,
(But o'er the downs a brooding shadow glides)
Untrampled flowers dream along the shore,
And Guthrum's galleys rust beneath the tides.

Now underneath this drowsy tree I lie
And turn old dreams upon my lazy knees,
Till ghostly giants fill the sumer sky
And phantom oars awake the sleeping seas.

Dreams Of Nineveh

Silver bridge in a broken sky,
  Golden fruit on a withered bough,
Red-lipped slaves that the ancients buy—
  What are the dreams of Nineveh now?

Ghostly hoofs in the brooding night
  Beat the bowl of the velvet stars.
Shadows of spears when the moon is white
  Cross the sands with ebony bars.

But not the shadows that brood her fall
  May check the sweep of the desert fire,
Nor a dead man lift up a crumbling wall,
  Nor a spectre steady a falling spire.

Death fires rise in the desert sky
  Where the armies of Sargon reeled;
And though her people still sell and buy,
  Nineveh's doom is set and sealed.

Silver mast with a silken sail,
  Sapphire seas 'neath a purple prow,
Hawk-eyed tribes on the desert trail—
  What are the dreams of Nineveh now?

By Robert E. Howard

Easter Island

How many weary centuries have flown
Since strange-eyed beings walked this ancient shore,
Hearing, as we, the green Pacific's roar,
Hewing fantastic gods from sullen stone!
The sands are bare; the idols stand alone.
Impotent 'gainst the years was all their lore:
They are forgot in ages dim and hoar;
Yet still, as then, the long tide-surges drone.

What dreams had they that shaped these uncouth
things?
Before these gods what victims bled and died?
What purple galleys swept along the strand
That bore the tribute of what dim sea-kings?
But now, they reign o'er a forgotten land,
Gazing forever out beyond the tide.

Empire's Destiny

Bab-ilu's women gazed upon our spears,
And roses flung, and sang to see us ride.
We built a glory for the marching years
And starred our throne with silver nails of pride.

Our horses' hoofs were shod with brazen fears:
We laved our hands in blood and iron tears,
And laughed to hear how shackled kings had died.

Our chariots awoke the sleeping world;
The thunder of our hoofs the mountains broke;
Before our spears were empires' banners furled
Amd death and doom and iron winds were hurled,
And slaughter rode before, and clouds and smoke--
Then in the desert lands the tribes awoke
And death and vengeance 'round our walls were
whirled.

Oh Babylon, lost Babylon! Where now
The opal altar and the golden spire,
The tower and the legend and the lyre?
Oh, withered fruit upon a broken bough!
The sobbing desert winds still whisper how
The sapphire city of the gods' desire
Fell in the smoke and crumbled in the fire;
And lizards bask upon her columns now.

Now poets sing her golden glory gone;
And Babylon has faded with the dawn.

By Robert E. Howard

Eternity

I am older than the world:
Older than life.
The race of man is a babe in the cradle of Time.
I am Alpha and Omega.

The first and the last;
The circle without end.
I am a serpent with its tail in its mouth;
I am a triangle whose tips overlap a circle.

I am the older sister of Destiny.
Before man was, I was:
And after man has vanished from the Universe, I will
be.
Time is a phantom, built by the mind of man;
There is no Time.
The thing that men call Time flies before my wind;
Time has beginning, duration, ending.
I am that which was, is and shall be;
Unceasing, Neverending, Eternal.
Number all the sands of all the shores of all the worlds
Of all the Universes.
And let each sand represent a million centuries;
And they all shall not be a single instant

Of Eternity.

For I am numberless and unnumbered,
Eternity had no beginning nor shall there be ending.
I am Alpha and Omega.
That which was, is and shall be;
Numberless and unnumbered.

Fables For Little Folk

He was six foot four and wide as a door
And he weighed two hundred pounds
And he laughed as he spoke, "I'll cool that bloke.
I'll flatten him in two rounds."
Ah, the crowd they cheered, but the crowd they jeered
When his foeman stepped in the ring;
They hissed and jowled and the giant scowled
And rushed with a round-house swing.
Yes, he came full tilt but the beans were spilt
For the smaller man timed him fair
And knocked him out with a left hand clout
And the crowd gave him the air.
So the moral is this: make your foeman miss
And never lead with your right,

By Robert E. Howard

But the first that you're to do is be sure
That it's not Jack Dempsey you fight.

Feach Air Muir Lionadhi Gealach Buidhe Mar Or

Mananan Mac Lir
   The son of the sea
   Is sib unto me
At the break of the year.

In the white autumn tides
   The ghost drums call
   When the midnights fall,
And the ghost ship rides
   Where the green waves crawl.

I break the loam
   By a Kerry hill—
   They beckon me still
 Through the purple gloom;
Strange eyes in the foam.

The sea-wind chills
   The crumbling stones,

And a ghost harp moans
In the shadowy hills.
But a white sail fills
    And a sweep-head drones.

The great white oars
    They gleam and bend
And the west wind roars
    From the blue world's end;
    They call me like a friend,
Forgotten shores.

Flaming Marble

I carved a woman out of marble when
The walls of Athens echoed to my fame,
And in the myrtle crown was shrined my name.
I wrought with skill beyond all mortal ken.
And into cold inhuman beauty then
I breathed a touch of white and living flame --
And from her pedestal she rose and came
To snare the souls and rend the hearts of men.

Without a soul, without a human heart
She shattered mortal love and mortal pride

And even I fell victim to my art,
With bitter joyless love I took my bride.
And still with frozen hate that never dies
She sits and stares at me with icy eyes.

Forbidden Magic

There came to me a Man one summer night,
When all the world lay silent in the stars,
And moonlight crossed my room with ghostly bars.
He whispered hints of weird, unhallowed sight;
I followed – then in waves of spectral light
Mounted the shimmery ladders of my soul
Where moon-pale spiders, huge as dragons, stole –
Great forms like moths, with wings of wispy white.

Around the world the sighing of the loon
Shook misty lakes beneath the false-dawn's gleams;
Rose tinted shone the sky-line's minaret;
I rose in fear, and then with blood and sweat
Beat out the iron fabrics of my dreams,
And shaped of them a web to snare the moon.

The Gates of Nineveh

These are the gates of Nineveh: here
Sargon came when his wars were won
Gazed at the turrets looming clear
Boldly etched in the morning sun

Down from his chariot Sargon came
Tossed his helmet upon the sand
Dropped his sword with its blade like flame
Stroked his beard with his empty hand

"Towers are flaunting their banners red
The people greet me with song and mirth
But a weird is on me," Sargon said
"And I see the end of the tribes of earth"

"Cities crumble, and chariots rust
I see through a fog that is strange and gray
All kingly things fade back to the dust
Even the gates of Nineveh"

By Robert E. Howard

Girl

Gods, what a handsome youth across the way.
  What shall I do to make him notice me?
I must not be too obvious—there
  I'll shift my dress, demurely and let him see
A quick glance of an ankle very trim;
  Then blush and smooth my skirts down hastily
As if 'twere unintentional—Hell!
  The fool's not even got his eyes on me.

A Great Man Speaks

They set me up on high, a marble saint,
  As if to guard the virtue of the park.
  My flanks are gaunt, my gaze is cold and stark,
For I must look the part the liars paint,
They've cleansed my history of fleshy taint.
  The elders bid the younger people mark
  How virtuous I gleam against the dark—
Could I but speak I'd make the bastards faint.

Great God, how could they know the lusty zest,
  The love of life that made my sinews dance?—
  Below me now, against my base, inert,

A lousy tramp, a sleeping house-maid rest,
  I yearn for that square flask in his old pants.
  My fingers burn to feel beneath her skirt.

The Harp of Alfred

I heard the harp of Alfred
As I went o'er the downs,
When thorn-trees stood at even
Like monks in dusky gowns;
I heard the music Guthrum heard
Beside the wasted towns:

When Alfred, like a peasant,
Came harping down the hill,
And the drunken danes made merry
With the man they sought to kill,
And the Saxon king laughed in their beards
And bent them to his will.

I heard the harp of Alfred
As the twilight waned to night;
I heard ghost armies tramping
As the dim stars flamed white;

And Guthrum walked at my left hand,
And Alfred at my right.

Illusion

(In Illusion, seeking to express myself in the clearest
manner possible, I have, for this effect, violated the
rules common of rhythm and poetry.)

I stood upon surf-booming cliffs
And heard the tide-race roaring, roaring strong and
deep and free;
On tall wind wings the white clouds sudded by.
Far to the eat the ocean met the sky
And the booming cliffs re-echoed to the thunder of
the sea.
Green are the waves and fringed with white the crest:
Strong colour contrasts, turquoise, sapphire, now.
Tumbling the jade green billows from the west
Roars the wild sea-wind. Keep your sea. I go.
Stranger to me the fierce red-blooded zest,
The wild beast urge, the primitive behest.
Fierce primal impulses are thoughts I do not know.
I've ever dwelt 'mid worlds of vaguer tone,
All tints and colors merging soft and dim,

No garish flare of reds at the desert's rim—
The sea-winds murmur there a pleasing drone;
The sea-fogs grace the ocean, friendly, grey.
'Mid soft-hued woodlands shy nymphs have their
play.
Ad so I'll none of all this garish joy,
These blazing dawns that leap like maids o'er-bold;
The flaming greens and reds and yellows cloy,
Barbaric tints of crimson, blazing gold.
The worlds I seek are like soft, golden chimes;
Soft merging tints that match the breeze's croon
And no false note plays in the world-scheme
rhymes—
I seek soft, vague plateaus of the moon.

Ivory in the Night

Maidens of star and of moon,
born from the mists of the age,
I thrill to the touch of your hands,
in the night when the shadows are o'er me.
Your eyes are like the gulfs of the night,
your limbs are like ivory gleaming—
But your lips are more red than is mortal,
and pointed the nails of your fingers.

By Robert E. Howard

Jack Dempsey

Through the California mountains
And many a wooded vale
The wind from seaward whispers
The name of the Nonpareil
O'er many a peak snow covered
O'er many a woodland fair
The sea-breeze murmurs the wonderful tale
Of the lad from County Clare.
But never the wind from seaward
And never the brooks of the vale
Can speak the half of the glory,
The due of the Nonpareil.

Champion of all Champions,
Greatest in all times' bound,
The lad who held Fitzsimmons
For thirteen gory rounds.
But the ring's red history passes
To a swiftly roving tale,
And there's few who now remember
The name of the Nonpareil.
But here's to the greatest of fighters,
To a name that never shall fail,

To the name of the first Jack Dempsey
The wonderful Nonpareil.

John L. Sullivan

Bellowing, blustering, old John L.
Fearing nothing 'tween sky and hell!
Rushing, roaring, swinging his right.
Smashing, crashing, forcing the fight.
Battering foes until they fell,
Tilt your glasses to old John L.!

Mitchell he knocked, from the ring clear out!
Dropped Kilrain with a single clout!
Laflin he beat and Burke he flayed,
Knocked out the Maori Giant, Slade!
Packed in each fist, damnation and hell!
Tilt your glasses to old John L.!

Old John L.'s in town today
He's hitting it down the Great White way.
Look at his swallow tail coat, silk hat!
Mustache too, say he's on a bat!
Living it in, that you can tell,
Tilt your glasses to old John L.!

By Robert E. Howard

He's cleaned out the roughest, toughest saloon,
He's licked O'Rourke and Jem McClune,
Sampled every saloon on the streets,
Buying drinks for all he meets,
He's taking the bowery in pell-mell!
Tilt your glasses to old John L.!

Stick in your head in the grog-shop door,
Look at him! Listen to his roar!
"Set out eh whiskey. Jimmy, ye bum!
Belly the bar, ye half bred scum!
I can lick any guy from here to hell!"
Tilt your glasses to old John L.!

The world moves on and the ring moves too
Old fighters have long given way to new.
But here;s a health to the olden days,
To the wild old, mad old, bad old ways,
When a fight was a fight and not a sell,
And tilt your glasses to old John L.

Kid Lavigne is Dead

Hang up the battered gloves; Lavigne is dead.
Bold and erect he went into the dark.
The crown is withered and the crowds are fled,
The empty ring stands bare and lone—yet hark:
The ghostly roar of many a phantom throng
Floats down the dusty years, forgotten long.

Hot blazed the lights above the crimson ring
Where there he reigned in his full prime, a king.
The throngs' acclaim roared up beneath their sheen
And whispered down the night: "Lavigne! Lavigne!"
Red splashed the blood and fierce the crashing blows.
Men staggered to the mat and reeling rose.
Crowns glittered there in splendour, won or lost,
And bones were shattered as the sledges crossed.

Swift as a leopard, strong and fiercely lean,
Champions knew the prowess of Lavigne.
The giant dwarf Joe Walcott saw him loom
And broken, bloody, reeled before his doom.
Handler and Everhardt and rugged Burge
Saw at the last his snarling face emerge
From bloody mists that veiled their dimming sight
Ere they sank down into unlighted night.

Strong men and bold, lay vanquished at his feet.
Mighty was he in triumph and defeat.
Far fade the echoes of the ringside's cheers
And all is lost in mists of dust-dead years.
Cold breaks the dawn; the East is ghastly red.
Hand up the broken gloves; Lavigne is dead.

The Kissing of Sal Snooboo

A bunch of the girls were whooping it up
In the old Lip-stick saloon,
And the kid at the player-piano
Was twanging a jazzy tune,
When out of the night with perfume on his shirt
And stacomb upon his hair,
A young man staggered inside the door
And meowed like a grizzly-bear.
He kicked the kid off the piano stool
And sat him down to play.
The piano yowled like an old tom cat
To the tune of "Hip! Hurray!"
Says he, "Gals, you don't know me,
But, by gosh, I know you,
And one of you is a classy dame,

37

And that one is Sal Snooboo!"

She squawked and somebody turned the lights,
Something went "Smack!" in the dark.
There was nothing for anybody to do
But to stand still and s****** and hark.
Somebody turned the lights on,
And Sally was standing there,
But the stranger wasn't; he was done,
And Sal was arranging her hair.

A Lady's Chamber

Orchid, jasmine and heliotrope
Scent the gloom where the dead men grope.

Silver, ruby-eyed leopards crouch
At the carven ends of the silken couch.

A purple mist of a perfume rare
Billows and sways, and weights the air.

The pale blue domes of the ceiling rise
Gemmed and carved like opium skies—
Golden serpents with crystal eyes.

Why should men grow strange and cold,
Like a marble heart in a breast of gold?

Their eyes are ice and they look strange tales,
They carve the mist with their long jade nails.

Orchid, jasmine and heliotrope
Scent the gloom where dead men grope;
They have stabbed their hearts with a golden sword
And hanged themselves with a silken rope.

Laughter

Laughter's the lure of the gods; therefore must ye
laugh
Mocking Destiny's nods, a strong wind driving the
chaff

Lesbia

From whence came this grim desire?
  What was the wine in my blood?
What raced through my veins like fire

And beat at my brain like a flood?

Bare is the desert's dust,
    Deep is the emerald sea—
Barer my deathless lust,
    Deeper the hunger of me.

Goddess I sit and brood—
    They cringe to my Hell-lit eyes,
The wretched women nude
    I have gripped between my thighs.

As they writhed between my hands
    And the ocean heard their screams
Firing my passion's brands
    As I dreamed my lurid dreams.

Their breath came fast and hot,
    Their tresses were Hades' mesh;
World and the worlds were not;
    Flesh against pulsing flesh.

Their white limbs fluttered and tossed,
    They whimpered beneath my grasp
And their maindenhood was lost
    In strange unnatural clasp.

By Robert E. Howard

Hours my pleasure beguiled
  The green Arcadian glades,
As idle mornings I whiled
  With free-hipped country maids.

Under the star-gemmed skies
  That looked upon curious scenes
I have spread the round white things
  Of naked and frightened queens.

What was it turned my face
  From brown-limbed Grecian boys,
Weary of their embrace
  To darker and barer joys?

A miser weary of coins
  I wearied of early charms,
Of youths who ungirt my loins,
  Restless sighed in their arms.

With many a youth I lay,
  But their wine to me was dregs.
I found scant joy in they
  Who parted my supple legs.

I turned to the loves I prize;
  Found joy amid perfumed curls,
In a maiden's amorous sighs,
  In the tears of naked girls.

These are the wine of delight—
  A girl's ungirdled charms,
A woman's laugh in the night
  As she lies in my eager arms.

Goddess I sit and laugh,
  Nude as the scornful moon—
World and the worlds are chaff
  Say, shall my day be soon?

Libertine

I set my soul to a wild lute
  And taught my feet to dance.
I float, a broken straw,
  Upon the Sea of Chance.

By Robert E. Howard

Life

They bruised my soul with a proverb,
They bruised my back with a rod,
And they bade me bow to my elders,
For that was the word of God.

They pent up my soul and bound me
Till life was a living death,
They struck the wine from my fingers,
The passion from my breath.

I reached my hands to living,
They hurled me back into school,
And they said, "Go learn your lessons,
"You innocent young fool."

They yowled till they woke the trumpets --
And the sword blade rent the plow,
And they said, "It is your duty
"To die for your elders now."

They cowered far from the battle
As I went to the strife,
And I spilled my guts in the trenches
In the red dawn of my life.

And the elders named me hero,
But more than their words and ire
Was the scent of a strange wild flower
There where I died in the mire.

Lines to G. B. Shaw

Oh, G.B.S., oh, G.B.S.,
You lousy son of a bitch,
You lift your yawp across the world
Like a bullfrog in a ditch.

I would that by foliage which
Your scholarly phizz thatches
Tied to a smoking stake you were
By a tribe of wild Apaches

You could deride them in that style
Of which you're so enamored,
While someone with a tomahawk
Your lordly cranium hammered.

And several thousand dancing braves,
The more the merrier,

Were sticking Spanish Daggers in
Your antequate posterior.

Lust

I am a golden lure.
I am the laughter of false goddesses.
I go disguised as Love.
Men are my slaves.
Women are my slaves.
I am a goddess and the world is my shrine.
I am the night wind
Blowing through the leaves.
I am the moonlight of a hidden glade.
I am starlight
On a palace.
I am Lust.

The Maiden of Kercheezer

She was snoozing on her sweezer,
  Many a goofish year ago,
And a smile was on her beezer,
  As she gently scratched her toe.

She, the Maiden of Kercheezer,
  Hair as black as a harness tug,
As is fluttered in the breezer,
  O'er her lovely, girlish mug.

Evening dress of green and yeller,
  What a shoulder she could shake
And she had a nifty feller,
  Hight the knight of Duckandrake.

He was knock-kneed, she was cross-eyed,
  Oh, they were a lovely pair,
How he'd fondly knock her hoss-eyed,
  As she gently pulled out his hair.

And her folks didn't like his beezer,
  But what difference did that make?
And the maiden of Kercheezer, ever
  Eloped with noble Duckandrake.

Miser's Gold

"Nay, have no fear. The man was blind," said she.
"How could he see 'twas we that took his gold?

"The devil, man! I thought you were bold!"
"This is a chancy business!" muttered he,
"And we'll be lucky if we get to sea.
"The fellow deals with demons, I've been told."
"Let's open the chest, shut up and take a hold."
Then silence as they knocked the hinges free.

A glint of silver and a sheen of jade—
Two strange gems gleaming from a silken fold—
Rare plunder – gods, was that a hidden blade?
A scream, a curse, two bodies stark and cold.
With jewel eyes above them crawled and swayed
The serpent left to watch the miser's gold.

Monarchs

These be kings of men,
Lords of the Ultimate Night,
Kings-of-the-desert and fen -
Jackal, vulture, and kite.

Moon Mockery

I walked in Tara's wood one summer night,
And saw, amid the still, star-haunted skies,
A slender moon in silver mist arise,
And hover on the hill as if in fright.
Burning, I seized her veil and held her tight:
An instant all her glow was in my eyes;
Then she was gone, swift as a white bird flies,
And I went down the hill in opal light.

And soon I was aware, as down I came,
That all was strange and new on every side;
Strange people went about me to and fro,
And when I spoke with trembling mine own name
They turned away, but one man said: "He died
In Tara Wood, a hundred years ago."

The Moor Ghost

They hauled him to the crossroads
As day was at its close;
They hung him to the gallows
And left him for the crows.

His hands in life were bloody,
His ghost will not be still
He haunts the naked moorlands
About the gibbet hill.

And oft a lonely traveler
Is found upon the fen
Whose dead eyes hold a horror
Beyond the world of men.

The villagers then whisper,
With accents grim and dour:
"This man has met at midnight
The phantom of the moor."

The Mountains of California

Grass and the rains and snow,
  Trumpet and tribal drum;
Across my crests the people go
  Over my peaks the people come.
Girt with the pelts of lion and hare.
  Plodding with oxen wains,
Climbing the steeps on a Spanish mare,
  Soaring in aeroplanes.

Men with their hates and their ires,
   Men with their loves and their lust
Still shall I reign when their spires
   And their castles tumble to dust.

Nun

I have anchored my ship to a quiet port;
   A land that is holy and blest.
But I gaze through my bars at the tempest's sport
   And I long for the sea's unrest.

Ocean-Thoughts

The strong winds whisper o'er the sea,
   Flinging the gray-gnarled ocean's spate;
The gray waves lash along the lea.

The lone gulls wings are high and free,
   The great seal trumpets for his mate;
The high winds drum, the wild winds dree.

The gray shoals roar unceasingly,
   Where combers march in kingly state,

The crest-crowned monarchs of the sea.

And now, along the lone, white lea,
  The surges fade, the winds abate.
And the wide sea lies silently.

But far to islands, restlessly
  Surges the tide, unreined and great,
Forever roaming and forever free.

And thus my soul, forever restlessly,
  Longs for the outworld, vast, unultimate,
The vasty freedom of the swinging sea,
Forever roaming and forever free.

The One Black Stain

They carried him out on the barren sand
where the rebel captains died;
Where the grim gray rotting gibbets stand
as Magellan reared them on the strand,
And the gulls that haunt the lonesome land
wail to the lonely tide.

Drake faced them all like a lion at bay,

with his lion head upflung:
"Dare ye my word of law defy,
to say this traitor shall not die?"
And his captains dared not meet his eye
but each man held his tongue.

Solomon Kane stood forth alone,
grim man of sober face:
"Worthy of death he may well be,
but the trial ye held was mockery,
"Ye hid your spite in a travesty
where justice hid her face.

"More of the man had ye been, on deck
your sword to cleanly draw
"In forthright fury from its sheath
and openly cleave him to the teeth --
"Rather than slink and hide beneath
a hollow word of the law."

Hell rose in the eyes of Francis Drake.
"Puritan knave!" swore he.
"Headsman! Give him the axe instead!
He shall strike off yon traitor's head!"
Solomon folded his arms and said,
darkly and somberly:

By Robert E. Howard

"I am no slave for your butcher's work."
"Bind him with triple strands!"
Drake roared and the men obeyed,
Hesitantly, as if afraid,
But Kane moved not as they took his blade
and pinioned his iron hands.

They bent the doomed man over to his knees,
the man who was to die;
They saw his lips in a strange smile bend,
one last long look they saw him send,
At Drake his judge and his one time friend
who dared not meet his eye.

The axe flashed silver in the sun,
a red arch slashed the sand;
A voice cried out as the head fell clear,
and the watchers flinched in sudden fear,
Though 'twas but a sea bird wheeling near
above the lonely strand.

"This be every traitor's end!"
Drake cried, and yet again.
Slowly his captains turned and went
and the admiral's stare was elsewhere bent

Than where the cold scorn with anger blent
in the eyes of Solomon Kane.

Night fell on the crawling waves;
the admiral's door was closed;
Solomon lay in the stenching hold;
his irons clashed as the ship rolled.
And his guard, grown weary and overbold,
lay down his pipe and dozed.

He woke with a hand at his corded throat
that gripped him like a vise;
Trembling he yielded up the key,
and the somber Puritan stood free,
His cold eyes gleaming murderously
with the wrath that is slow to rise.

Unseen, to the admiral's door,
went Solomon Kane from the guard,
Through the night and silence of the ship,
the guard's keen dagger in his grip;
No man of the dull crew saw him slip
through the door unbarred.

Drake at the table sat alone,
his face sunk in his hands;

By Robert E. Howard

He looked up, as from sleeping --
but his eyes were blank with weeping
As if he saw not, creeping,
death's swiftly flowing sands.

He reached no hand for gun or blade
to halt the hand of Kane,
Nor even seemed to hear or see,
lost in black mists of memory,
Love turned to hate and treachery,
and bitter, cankering pain.

A moment Solomon Kane stood there,
the dagger poised before,
As a condor stoops above a bird,
and Francis Drake spoke not nor stirred
And Kane went forth without a word
and closed the cabin door.

One Blood Strain

Now autumn comes and summer goes,
　And rises in my heart again,
As witchfire glimmers through a pool,
　The mystic madness of the Dane.

Blue thunder of a foaming sea
   Reverberating through my sleep,
White billowing sails that fill and flee
   Across a wind-swept restless deep—

They speak to me with subtle tongue
   Of blue-bright ways my forbears trod,
When time the bearded Vikings bent
   Their oars against the winds of God.

And I am but a common man
   Who treads a dreary way ashore,
But oceans thunder in my dreams,
And blue waves break on creaking beams,
And foaming water swirls and creams
   About the strongly bending oar.

When summer goes and autumn comes
   To paint the leaves with sombre fires,
I feel, like throbs of distant drums,
   The urge of distant nameless sires.

By Robert E. Howard

One Who Comes at Eventide

I think when I am old a furtive shape
Will sit beside me at my fireless hearth,
Dabbled with blood from stumps of severed wrists,
And flacked with blackened bits of mouldy earth.

My blood ran fire when the deed was done;
Now it runs colder than the moon that shone
On shattered fields where dead men lay in heaps
Who could not hear a ravished daughter's moan.

(Dim through the bloody dawn on bitter winds
The throbbing of the distant guns was brought
When I reeled like a drunkard from the hut
That hid the horror my red hands had wrought.)

So now I fire my veins with stinging wine,
And hoard my youth as misers hug their gold,
Because I know what shape will come and sit
Beside my crumbling hearth - when I am old.

Poet

My soul is a blaze
Of passionate desire;
My soul is a blaze
That sets my pen on fire.

Private Magrath of the A.E.F

(As an aid to remembrance of November 11th, 1918)

The night was dark as a Harlem coon
Smoke and clounds once lin' the moon;
Flares goin' up with a venomous sound,
Bustin' and throwin' a green light around.
An', yeah, there was me cursin' my soul
For losin' meself from the raidin' patrol.
Creepin' along in the mud and the slime,
Cussin' and havin' the Devil's own time.
Smeared and spattered with Flanders mire,
Tearin' me clothes on the loose barbwire.

I'm crawlin' along, keepin' close to the ground,
When all of a sudden I hears me a sound.
I halt and I listen, it's too dark for sight

But some bird's ahead of me there in the night.
I reached for my gun—then I swear through me teeth
For somewhere the thing's fallen out of its sheath.
But before I can move, I hear feet a-slush
And something to meself: "Come right ahead Fritz,
I've lost me gat but I've got me mitts."

I sidestep quick as he makes his spring,
His bay'net flashes, I duck, I swing!
Flush on the jaw my right he stops,
Down in the muck on his face he flops.
I'm cursin' him for a bloody Hun
As I loosen the bay'net off his gun.
I feel for his ribs 'neath his tunic drab
For I've only time for a single stab.
I feel a locket a-danglin there,
I jerk it out, then a rockets flare

Limns it in light like crimson flame
And I see the face of a white haired dame
And German letters beneath it run,
Which I take to mean "To my darlin' son."
I haul that Hun up onto his pegs,
And I says, "Get goin'; and shake your legs.
Your line are that way, now get gone."
And I hends him a boot to help him on.

Saying, "Make tracks on your homeward path,
With the compliments of Monk Magrath."

Prude

I dare not join my sisters in the street;
   I think of people's talk, the cynic stare.
Fierce envy makes me scornful of their play,
   And hide my lust behind a haughty air.

Rebellion

The marble statues tossed against the sky
   In gestures blind as though to rend and kill,
   Not one upon his pedestal was still.
Stiff fingers clutched at winds that whispered by,
And from the white lips rose a deathly cry:
   "Cursed be the hands that broke us from the hill!
   There slumber of unbirth was ours till
The gave us life that cannot live or die."

And then as from a dream I stirred and woke—
   Sublime and still each statue raised its head,
   Etched pure and cold against the leafy green,

No limb was moved, no sigh the silence broke;
  And people walked amid the grove and said:
  "How peaceful these white gods!—aye, how serene."

Red Thunder

Thunder in the black skies beating down the rain,
Thunder in the black cliffs, looming o'er the main,
Thunder on the black sea and thunder in my brain.

God's on the night wind, Satan's on his throne
By the red lake lurid and great grim stone–
Still through the roofs of Hell the brooding thunders
drone.

Trident for a rapier, Satan thrusts and foins
Crouching on his throne with his great goat loins–
Souls are his footstools and hearts are his coins.

Slave of all the ages, though lord of the air;
Solomon o'ercame him, set him roaring there,
Crouching on the coals where the great flames flare.

Thunder from the grim gulfs, out of cosmic deep
Where the red eyes glimmer and the black wings

sweep,
Thunder down to Satan, wake him from his sleep!

Thunder on the shores of Hell, scattering the coal,
Riding down the mountain on the moon-mare's foal,
Blasting out the caves of the gnome and the troll.

Satan, brother Satan, rise and break your chain!
Solomon is dust and his spells grow vain–
Rise through the world in the thunder and the rain.

Rush upon the cities, roaring in your might,
Break down the towers in the moon's pale light,
Build a wall of corpses for God's great sight,
Quench the red thunder in my brain this night.

Repentance

How is it that I am what I am
   How did I come to fall?
Who was the man my soul to damn
   Black in the sight of all?
Who was it came in my virgin hood
   And in some evil hour
Turned all my life to bad from good

Bruising the tender flower?
I cannot remember the fellow's name
　I had long ago forgot;
I was young and my blood was flame
　The person mattered not.
I was hot as a blazing brand
　Blood and body and nerve
Ripe to be plucked by the first man's hand
　And any man would serve.
I have had my day, I have had my fling
　Men have bowed at my knee.
I sit in the bars where the harlots sing
　To sailors hot from the sea.
Sallow my cheeks and my lips have faded
　Life's roses slip my clutch
But my blood is still hot and still unjaded
　I can thrill to the deck-hand's touch.
Still I thrill to the hands of men
　I love the contact yet
The breath that is laden with wharfside gin
　The scent of tobacco and sweat.
Bristly jowls on my painted cheek
　The obscene, whispered jest,
Calloused hands that lustfully seek
　My out-worn charms to quest.
My by-gone life is dim and far;

I am content with gin,
A slug of wine, sometimes at the bar,
  A room for the sailormen.

The Riders of Babylon

The riders of Babylon clatter forth
Like the hawk-winged scourgers of Azrael
To the meadow-lands of the South and North
And the strong-walled cities of Israel.
They harry the men of the caravans,
They bring rare plunder across the sands
To deck the throne of the great god Baal.
But Babylon's king is a broken shell
And Babylon's queen is a sprite from Hell;
And men shall say, "Here Babylon fell,"
Ere Time has forgot the tale.
The riders of Babylon come and go
From Gaza's halls to the shores of Tyre;
They shake the world from the lands of snow
To the deserts, red in the sunset's fire;
Their horses swim in a sea of gore
And the tribes of the earth bow down before;
They have chained the seas where the Cretans sail.
But Babylon's sun shall set in blood;

Her towers shall sink in a crimson flood;
And men shall say, "Here Babylon stood,"
Ere Time forgot the tale.

The Ride of Falume

Falume of Spain rode forth amain when twilight's
crimson fell
To drink a toast with Bahram's ghost in the scarlet
land of Hell.
His rowels clashed as swift he dashed along the
flaming skies;
The sunset rode at his bridle braid and the moon was
in his eyes.
The waves were green with an eerie sheen over the
hills of Thule
And the ripples beat to his horse's feet like a serpent in
a pool.
On vampire wings the shadow things wheeled round
and round his head,
Till he came at last to a kingdom vast in the Land of
the Restless Dead.

They thronged about in a grisly rout, they caught at
his silver rein;

"Avaunt, foul host! Tell Bahram's ghost Falume has
come from Spain!"
Then flame-arrayed rose Bahram's shade: "What
would ye have, Falume?"
"Ho, Bahram who on earth I slew where Tagus' waters
boom,
Now though I shore your life of yore amid the
burning West,
I ride to Hell to bid ye tell where I might ride to rest.
My beard is white and dim my sight and I would fain
be gone.
Speak without guile: where lies the isle of mystic
Avalon?"

"A league beyond the western wind, a mile beyond the
moon,
Where the dim seas roar on an unknown shore and
the drifting stars lie strewn;
The lotus buds there scent the woods where the quiet
rivers gleam,
And king and knight in the mystic light the ages
drowse and dream."

With sudden bound Falume wheeled round, he fled
through the flying wrack
Till he came again to the land of Spain with the sunset

at his back.
"No dreams for me, but living free, red wine and
battle's roar;
I breast the gales and I ride the trails until I ride no
more."

The Robes of the Righteous

I am a saintly reformer,
   basking in goodly reknown
Sure of applaud of the righteous,
   cinctured in purity's gown.
Young men and old men revere me,
   women and girls out of school
Come to me telling their secrets,
   seeking my counseling cool.
Little they know of my story
   when I was the water-front's toast.
Back in the days of my glory
   down on the Barbary Coast.
Young and my lips full and crimson,
   flaming with passionate blood,
My love was the leap of an ocean,
   my passion the swing of the flood.
Changing and varied my fancies

yet no woman ever gave more
For I joyed in the man on my body
   just as much as the one just before
Ah, nights that were lurid and gorgeous,
   under the bar lamps blaze
Flutter of cars on the table,
   faces that leered through the haze
Of smoke drifting up from the stogies,
   the red liquor flowing free
And the shout of the salty ballass
   that sailors sang from the sea.
The money scattered like water,
   the pagan thrill of the dance
The hand that groped in my clothing,
   the burning and meaning glance
Then the look as the stair I mounted,
   the man that left the floor,
The joyous and panting waiting,
   the stealthy knock at my door—
What if they knew, the elders,
   that I was a Barbary whore?
Hiding my charms with meekness
   under purity's gown
Sure of applaud of the righteous,
   basking in goodly reknown.

A Roman Lady

There is a strangeness in my soul
  A dark and brooding sea.
Nor all the waves on Capri's shoal
  Might stay the thirst of me.
For men have come and men have gone
  For pleasure or for hire.
Though they lay broken at the dawn
  They did not quench my fire.
My pity is a deathly ruth
  I burn men with my eyes.
Oh, would all men were one strong youth
  To break between my thighs.
Any many a man his fortune spread
  To glut my ecstacy
As I lay panting on his bed
  In shameless nudity.
But all of ancient Egypt's gold
  Can never equal this,
Nor all the treasures kingdoms hold,
  A single hour of bliss.
Within my villa's high domain
  Are boys from Britain's rocks
And dark eyed slender lads from Spain
  And Greeks with perfumed locks.

And youths of soft and subtle speech
  From furtherest Orient,
Wherever arms of legions reach
  And Roman chains are sent.
Why may I not be satiate
  With kisses of some boy—
They only rouse my passions spate
  I never know such joy
As when through chambers filled with noise
  Of wails and pleas and sighs
I stride among my naked boys
  With whips that bruise their thighs.
I drift through mists red flaming flung
  On hills of ecstacies
As shoulder-wealed and buttock-stung
  They shriek and kiss my knees.

Romance

I am king of all the Ages
I am ruler of the stars
I am master of Time's pages
And I mock at chain and bars.
Now, as when I sailed the world
Ere the galley's sails were furled

And the barnacles had crusted on their spars.

I am strife, I am Life,
I am mistress, I am wife!
I am wilder than the sea wind, I am fiercer than the
fire!
I am tale and song and fable, I am Akkad, I am Babel,
I am Calno, I am Carthage, I am Tyre!

For I walked the streets of Gaza
   when the world was wild and young,
And I reveled in Carchemish when the golden
minstrels sung;
All the world-road was my path, as I sang the songs of
Gath
Or trod the streets of Nineveh where harlots roses
flung.

I swam the wide Euphrates
   where it wanders through the plain
And I saw the dawn come flaming over Tyre.
I walked the roads of Ammon
   when the hills were veiled in rain,
And I watched the stars anon from the walls of
Askalon
And I rose the plains of Palestine beneath the

dawning's fire
When the leaves upon the trees danced
   and fluttered in the breeze
And a slim girl of Juda went singing to a lyre.

Roundelay Of The Roughneck

Let others croon of lover's moon,
Of roses, birds on wing,
Maidens, the waltz's dreaming tune,—
Of strong thewed deeds I sing.

Let poets seek the tinted reek,
Perfume of ladies gay,
Of winds of wild outlands I speak,
The lash of far sea spray.

Of dear swamp brakes, of storm whipped lakes,
Dank jungle, reedy fen,
Of seas the pound the plunging strakes,
Of men and deeds of men.

Prospector; king of the battling ring;
Tarred slave of tide's behests,
Monarchs of muscle shall I sing,

By Robert E. Howard

Lords of the hairy chests.

Though some may stay 'neath cities away,
To toil with maul and hod,
To outer trails most take their way,
To lands yet scarcely trod.

The torrent's might, the dizzy height,
Shall never bate their breath,
With desert's toils they match their might,
And hurl their mocks at Death.

The tropic creek, the jungle reek
That steams through sullen trees,
The boding wild where leopards shriek
Holds never fear for these.

Nor do they shrink from hell's own brink,
When kites low wheeling fly,
And circling near the jackals slink,
And sands stretch bare to sky.

Far swing their trails through calms and gales,
From Polar sea to Horn,
From bleak ice-glittering peaks and vales,
To sun-kissed seas of morn.

In driving snow, where artic floe
Surges though ice-reft straits,
Where bergs sweep southward, row on row,
And wind fiends shriek their hates.

Where the broad sun smiles on a hundred isles
With the long sea reach between,
And the lone gull wheels for a thousand miles,
And the reefs lift fanged and lean.

On Polar trails where the screeching gales
Bellow and roar and blow,
And the skies are gone while the fierce wind rails,
And the path fades in the snow.

By atolls lean where ships careen,
In the sullen, still lagoon.
And crouching bushman's spear is a sheen
In the light of the shuddering moon.

In the marshy swamp, in the jungle damp,
Tall trees in marching lines,
That echo again to the tusker's tramp,
Where the tiger glides through the vines.

By Robert E. Howard

On mountains bleak, on cliff and peak,
From Pole to Pole and Line,
Adventure still they ever seek,
Adventure still they find.

Rules of Etiquette

Rule I.
ALWAYS BE POLITE
If a girl stops you to talk while you are chasing your trains,
And it looks like they're going to lose ye,
Just up with your musket and knock out her brains,
Saying, "Miss, you'll have to excuse me."

Rule II.
NEVER BE RUDE
IF a tiresome guy should happen to call,
And stay and stay without leaving at all,
Just heave him out of the door on his dome,
And maybe he'll take the hint and go home.

Rule III.
BE CONSIDERATE OF LADIES
If you were going down the street,

And a pretty girl you chance to meet,
Don't hit her if she should you slight,
A swiftish kick is more polite.

Rule IV.
EXAMPLES
There was a guy named McDoodles,
With a face like an Austrian poodle's,
When folks said, "What a beeze--
You big piece of cheese!"
Why, he'd wallop them all on their noodles.

Rule V.
BE COURTEOUS
When a tailor's solicitor calls at your door,
Don't make him a greeting with your forty-four;
Don't give him a scowl and a horrible glare,
And say, "You poor fish! You bum! Take the air!"

He may be a bum and he may be a boob,
But it's none of your business if he's even a rube.
He's a human, although he may not look the part,
Either give him some clothes or a good running start.

Sailor

I saw a mermaid sporting in the bay,
  Far down, far down where blew no roaring gale;
About her snowy shoulders flashed the spray,
  The waves played emerald at her sinewy tail;
She swam a jade and golden, star-set way,
Where all the rainbow colors seemed to play—
  She vanished at the Swedish captain's hail
  Who bid me go to Hell and furl a sail.

The Sands of Time

Slow sift the sands of Time; the yellowed leaves
Go drifting down an old and bitter wind;
Across the frozen moors the hedges stand
In tattered garments that the frost have thinned.

A thousand phantoms pluck my ragged sleeve,
Wan ghosts of souls long into darkness thrust.
Their pale lips tell lost dreams I thought mine own,
And old sick longings smite my heart to dust.

I may not even dream of jeweled dawns,
Nor sing with lips that have forgot to laugh.

I fling aside the cloak of Youth and limp
A withered man upon a broken staff.

The Sea

The sea, the sea, the rolling sea!
High flung, wide swinging, so wild and free,
The leaping waves with their white-capped crest
The plunge and lunge on the ocean's breats
Like wild, white horses racing free,
With the swing of the rolling, surging sea!
The white sea cloud that drifts like a dream;
'The sea-gulls that skim o'er the waves, and scream;
The dolphin's plunge and the petrel's nest,
That is borne to land on the tide-race crest:
And all that goes, from mid-ocean to lea,
To make up the rolling, the surginf sea!
Can ye stand on the peaceful, quiet lea,
And gaze on the tumbling, tossing sea,
Out o'er the surge and the white waves' crest,
Nor feel a longing within your breast?
A drawing, a pull, be it day or night,
That tempts ye to dare the ocean's might.
I stood on the deck of a ship offshore
And harked to the awesome and deafening roar

By Robert E. Howard

Of the ocean waves when theys truck the reefs,
High tossed on the tide like crested chiefs
Whose plumes toss high 'bove the battling hordes,
Where leap the lances and flash the swords.
And the mighty waves rose high and steep
To the hand of the waves that smote the deep.
And my soul leaped wildm and my would leaped free,
To the leap and the swing of the rolling sea!
And my soul was freed with that ocean leap,
And it plumed the depths of the mighty deep!
Down, down, down where the mermaids ride,
Down where the things of the deep sea glide.
Down where the ships, long sunken, float,
War-ship and galley and coracle boat;
Down beyond reach of the storms or the tides,
To the coral halls where old Triton hides!
And I saw the mermaids and the mermen play,
The the kraken and sea-serpent locked in fray.
And all the ocean-marvels that be,
And the wonderful monsters of the sea.
I wandered 'mongst beautiful sea-flowers,
Where the castle built by the polyp towers,
Where the waters glitter with strange sea-jade,
And the sea-things swim through the deep-sea glade.
And then my soul came back on me,
Back through the surge of the swinging sea.

But still I gaze from the quiet lea,
And long for the swing of the plunging sea.

Secrets

There is a serpent lifts his crest o' nights
And hisses in the darkness of my room.
His substance and the cloaking night are one;
His form is of the soft, thick, musky dark.
His strange eyes glimmer and his scales are loud
Yet none but I can hear—and scarcely I.
His gliding whispers shake my sluggish soul
With strange wild fires and lights of other dreams.
He loops himself about me in the dark;
I struggle with a strange, wild ecstasy
And seek, yet would not wish, to free my limbs.
Strange shudders shake my limbs at his cold touch
As coil on coil he laps my naked form.
Colder than ice he is, yet in my soul
He kindles fires more hot that Hades' breath.
With soft insidious whisper at my cheek
He lures me to the midnight's curious joys.
I rise and follow. All the land is still.
the crescent moon hangs breathless in the sky,
Whose crystal deeps are pierced with pointed stars.

By Robert E. Howard

Through woodlands silver black he leads me on.
Over the terraced swards where fountains dance,
Until the moon lights up a window sill.
My naked feet no hint of sound may make.
We glide together o'er the silver sill.
I hear the velvet hangings swish behind
like whisper of some crimson nightmare's wings.
My feet sink deep in rugs of silken weave
And like a ghost I bend above the bed,
A girl lies there, her sleeping lips a-smile
On soft arm pillowing the golden head.
Her tender limbs stretched out in light repose.
There is no gown to veil her symmetry.
She lies and shimmers ivory in the moon.
Those perfect, scarlet lips were made to kiss;
My arm should be about that slender waist.
But here the serpent rustles grisly scales.
And sways beside me like a fearful tree.
His whispers speak of deeper, fiercer lusts,
Of wilder joys, most terrible and strange.
That change soft dreams to nightmares red and grim.
He indicates the curves of that soft breast;
He whispers of the red wine which is blood.
He makes me feel the thrill that's born of death.
This is not earthly—from what darkened world,
What shadowed planet, what inhuman sphere

Come such wild dreams, such fearsome fantasies?
The serpent bids me stoop to that soft breast
To let the dagger kiss—with one swift thrust—
Death should be beautiful, then crouching by
Watch with quick breath and glinting eye the blood
Drain slowly from that soft, rose-tinted cheek
Until the wine has oozed from every vein
Leaving her marble white and marble cold
Like some inhuman goddess from a star.
Drained clean of all the grosser things of life.
Then raise her gently from the ruby lake
And kiss her cheeks as one who knows true sin.

Serpent

I am the symbol of Creation and Destruction
I am the beginning and the end.
With my tail in my mouth
I am the Circle of Eternity.
Wisdom is in my eyes
And the dusk of wisdom lurks amid my coils.
My track circles the world
And I loop my coils around the Universe.
My head waves among the stars
And the nations fall prostrate before me.

Coiled, head upright, I am the spirit of the sea.
The world-shaking dinosaur was my henchman
And the flying dragons were my footmen.
The ancients knew me.
They reared shrines and altars
And I taught them dim, dusky wisdom.
I coiled in the ruins of Troy and Babylon
And on the forgotten streets of Nineveh.
The Norse called me Midgaard and built their galleys
Like a sea-serpent.
The Egyptians and the Indians called me Ysis
And the Phoenecians Baal.
I am the sea that girdles the world.
I am the first and I shall be the last.
I am the Serpent of the Ages.

Shadow of Dreams

Stay not from me that veil of dreams that gives
Strange seas and and skies and lands and curious fire,
Black dragons, crimson moons and white desire,
That through the silvery fabric sifts and sieves
Strange shadows, shades and all unmeasured things,
And in the sifting lends them shapes and wings
And makes them known in ways past common

knowing--
Red lands, black seas and ivory rivers flowing.

How of the gold we gather in our hands?
It cheers, but shall escape us at the last,
And shall mean less, when this brief day is past,
Than that we gathered on the yellow sands,
The phantom ore we found in Wizard-lands.

Keep not from me my veil of curious dreams
Through which I see the giant things which drink
From mountain-castled rivers--on the brink
Black elephants that woo the fronded streams,
And golden tom-toms pulsing through the dusk,
And yellow stars, black trees and red-eyed cats,
And bales of silk and amber jars of musk,
And opal shrines and tents and vampire bats.

Long highways climbing eastward to the moon,
And caravans of camels lade with spice,
And ancient sword hilts carved with scroll and rune,
And marble queens with eyes of crimson ice.

Uncharted shores where moons of scarlet spray
Break on a Viking's galley on the sand,
And curtains held by one slim silver band

That float from casements opening on a bay,
And monstrous iron castles, dragon-barred,
And purple cloaks with inlaid gems bestarred.

Long silver tasseled mantles, curious furs,
And camel bells and dawns and golden heat,
And tuneful rattle of the horseman's spurs
Along some sleeping desert city's street.

Time strides and all too soon shall I grow old
With still all earth to see, all life to live:
Then come to me, my silver veil, and sieve,
Seas of illusion beached with magic gold.

Skulls and Dust

The Persian slaughtered the Apis Bull;
    (Ammon-Ra is a darksome king.)
And the brain fermented beneath his skull.
    (Egypt's curse is a deathly thing.)

He rode on the desert raider's track;
    (Ammon-Ra is a darksome king.)
No man of his gleaming hosts came back.
And the dust winds drifted sombre and black.

(Egypt's curse is a deathly thing.)

The eons passed on the desert land;
    (Ammon-Ra is a darksome king.)
And a stranger trod the shifting sand.
    (Egypt's curse is a deathly thing.)

His idle hand disturbed the dead;
    (Ammon-Ra is a darksome king.)
Till he found Cambysses' skull of dread
Whence the frenzied brain so long had fled,
That once held terrible visions red.
    (Egypt's curse is a deathly thing.)

And an asp crawled from the dust inside
    (Ammon-Ra is a darksome king.)
And the stranger fell and gibbered and died.
    (Egypt's curse is a deathly thing.)

The Skull in the Clouds

The Black Prince scowled above his lance, and wrath
in his hot eyes lay,
"I would rather you rode with the spears of France
and not at my side today.

"A man may parry an open blow, but I know not
where to fend;
"I would that you were an open foe, instead of a
sworn friend.

"You came to me in an hour of need, and your heart I
thought I saw;
"But you are one of a rebel breed that knows not king
or law.
"You -- with your ever smiling face and a black heart
under your mail—
"With the haughty strain of the Norman race and the
wild, black blood of the Gael.

"Thrice in a night fight's close-locked gloom my shield
by merest chance
"Has turned a sword that thrust like doom—I wot
'twas not of France!
"And in a dust-cloud, blind and red, as we charged the
Provence line
"An unseen axe struck Fitzjames dead, who gave his
life for mine.

"Had I proofs, your head should fall this day or ever I
rode to strife.
"Are you but a wolf to rend and slay, with naught to

guide your life?
"No gleam of love in a lady's eyes, no honor or faith
or fame?"
I raised my faces to the brooding skies and laughed
like a roaring flame.

"I followed the sign of the Geraldine from Meath to
the western sea
"Till a careless word that I scarcely heard bred hate in
the heart of me.
"Then I lent my sword to the Irish chiefs, for half of
my blood is Gael,
"And we cut like a sickle through the sheafs as we
harried the lines of the Pale.

"But Dermod O'Connor, wild with wine, called me a
dog at heel,
"And I cleft his bosom to the spine and fled to the
black O'Neil.
"We harried the chieftains of the south; we shattered
the Norman bows.
"We wasted the land from Cork to Louth; we
trampled our fallen foes.

"But Conn O'Neill put on me a slight before the
Gaelic lords,

"And I betrayed him in the night to the red
O'Donnell swords.
"I am no thrall to any man, no vassal to any king.
"I owe no vow to any clan, nor faith to any thing.

"Traitor—but not for fear or gold, but the fire in my
own dark brain;
"For the coins I loot from the broken hold I throw to
the winds again.
"And I am true to myself alone, through pride and the
traitor's part.
"I would give my life to shield your throne, or rip
from your breast, the heart.

"For a look or a word, scarce thought or heard, I
follow a fading fire.
"Past bead and bell and the hangman's cell, like a
harp-call of desire.
"I may not see the road I ride for the witch-fire lamps
that gleam;
"But phantoms glide at my bridle-side, and I follow a
nameless Dream."

The Black Prince shuddered and shook his head, then
crossed himself amain:
"Go, in God's name, and never," he said, "ride in my

sight again."

The starlight silvered my bridle-rein; the moonlight
burned my lance
As I rode back from the wars again through the
pleasant hills of France,
As I rode to tell Lord Amory of the dark Fitzgerald
line
If the Black Prince dies, it needs must be by another
hand than mine.

Solomon Kane's Homecoming

The white gulls wheeled above the cliffs, the air was
slashed with foam,
The long tides moaned along the strand when
Solomon Kane came home.
He walked in silence strange and dazed through the
little Devon town,
His gaze, like a ghost's come back to life, roamed up
the streets and down.

The people followed wonderingly to mark his spectral
stare,
And in the tavern silently they thronged about him

there.

He heard as a man hears in a dream the worn old rafters creak,

And Solomon lifted his drinking-jack and spoke as a ghost might speak:

"There sat Sir Richard Grenville once; in smoke and flame he passed.

"And we were one to fifty-three, but we gave them blast for blast.

"From crimson dawn to crimson dawn, we held the Dons at bay.

"The dead lay littered on our decks, our masts were shot away.

"We beat them back with broken blades, till crimson ran the tide;

"Death thundered in the cannon smoke when Richard Grenville died.

"We should have blown her hull apart and sunk beneath the Main."

The people saw upon his wrist the scars of the racks of Spain.

"Where is Bess?" said Solomon Kane. "Woe that I caused her tears."

"In the quiet churchyard by the sea she has slept these seven years."
The sea-wind moaned at the window-pane, and Solomon bowed his head.
"Ashes to ashes, dust to dust, and the fairest fade," he said.

His eyes were mystical deep pools that drowned unearthly things,
And Solomon lifted up his head and spoke of his wanderings.
"Mine eyes have looked on sorcery in dark and naked lands,
"Horror born of the jungle gloom and death on the pathless sands.

"And I have known a deathless queen in a city old as Death,
"Where towering pyramids of skulls her glory witnesseth.
"Her kiss was like an adder's fang, with the sweetness Lilith had,
"And her red-eyed vassals howled for blood in that City of the Mad.

"And I have slain a vampire shape that sucked a black

king white,
"And I have roamed through grisly hills where dead men walked at night.
"And I have seen heads fall like fruit in a slaver's barracoon,
"And I have seen winged demons fly all naked in the moon.

"My feet are weary of wandering and age comes on apace;
"I fain would dwell in Devon now, forever in my place."
The howling of the ocean pack came whistling down the gale,
And Solomon Kane threw up his head like a hound that sniffs the trail.

A-down the wind like a running pack the hounds of the ocean bayed,
And Solomon Kane rose up again and girt his Spanish blade.
In his strange cold eyes a vagrant gleam grew wayward and blind and bright,
And Solomon put the people by and went into the night.

A wild moon rode the wild white clouds, the waves in white crests flowed,
When Solomon Kane went forth again and no man knew his road.
They glimpsed him etched against the moon, where clouds on hilltop thinned;
They heard an eery echoed call that whistled down the wind.

A Song of Cheer

The lords of Greenwich sallied forth
The men, also the maids;
The dames had cut and combed their hair,
The men wore theirs in braids.

They came unto a comrade's room,
They laid on him their hands
Said they, "Oh fiend, oh cringing wretch!
"Behold the traitor stands!"

They punched him thrice upon the nose,
They blacked his gleaming eye;
They nailed his trousers to the wall
And left him there to die.

But people came and cut him down
And gave him other pants.
"And tell us now," the people said
"How this thing came to chance?"

"Alas for me!" the wretch replied,
"My sinful lust for gold!
"My former friends are down on me—
I wrote a book that sold!"

The Song of the Bats

The dusk was on the mountain
And the stars were dim and frail
When the bats came flying, flying
From the river and the vale
To wheel against the twilight
And sing their witchy tale.

"We were kings of old!" they chanted,
"Rulers of a world enchanted;
"Every nation of creation
"Owned our lordship over men.
"Diadems of power crowned us,

"Then rose Solomon to confound us,
"In the form of beasts he bound us,
"So our rule was broken then."

Whirling, wheeling into westward,
Fled they in their phantom flight;
Was it but a wing-beat music
Murmured through the star-gemmed night?
Or the singing of a ghost clan
Whispering of forgotten might?

Sonora to Del Rio

Sonora to Del Rio is a hundred barren miles
Where the sotol weave and shimmer in the sun—
Like a host of swaying serpents straying down the bare
defiles
When the silver, scarlet webs of dawn are spun.

There are little 'dobe ranchoes, brooding far along the
sky
On the sullen, dreary bosoms of the hills.
Not a wolf to break the quiet, not a single bird to fly;
Where the silence is so utter that it thrills.

Maybe, in the heat of evening, comes a wind from
Mexico
Laden with the heat of seven Hells,
And the rattler in the yucca and the buzzard dark and
slow
Hear and understand the grisly tales it tells.

Gaunt and stark and bare and mocking rise the
everlasting cliffs
Like a row of sullen giants carved of stone,
Till the traveler, mazed with silence, thinks to look at
hieroglyphs,
Thinks to see a carven pharaoh on his throne.

And the road goes on forever, o'er the barren hill
forever,
And there's little to hint of flowing wine—
But beyond the hills and sotol there's a mellow
curving river
And a land of sun and mellow wine.

Surrender

I will rise some day when the day is done
And the stars begin to quiver;

I will follow the road of the setting sun
Till I come to a dreaming river.

I am weary now of the world and vow
Of the winds and the winter weather;
I'll reel through a few more years somehow,
Then I'll quite them altogether.

I'll go to a girl that once I knew
And I will not swerve or err,
And I care not if she be false or true
For I am not true to her.

Her eyes are fierce and her skin is brown
And her wild blood hotly races,
But it's little I care if she does not frown
At any man's embraces.

Should I ask for a love none may invade?
Is she more or less than human?
Do I ask for more, who have betrayed
Man, devil, god and woman?

Enough for me if she has of me
A bamboo hut she'll share,
And enough tequilla to set me free

From the ghosts that leer and stare.

I'll lie all day in a sodden sleep
Through days without name or number,
With only the wind in the sky's blue deep
To haunt my unshaken slumber.

And I'll lie by night in the star-roofed hut
Forgetful and quiet hearted,
Till she comes with her burning eyes half shut
And her red lips hot and parted.

The past is flown when the cup is full,
And there is no chain for linking
And any woman is beautiful
When a man is blind with drinking.

Life is a lie that cuts like a knife
With its sorrow and fading blisses;
I'll go to a girl who asks naught of life
Save wine and a drunkard's kisses.

No man shall know my race or name,
Or my past sun-ripe or rotten,
Till I travel the road by which I came,
Forgetting and soon forgotten.

Tarantella

Heads! Heads! Heads!

Bounce on the cobble stones.

Glitter of scarlets and flame of reds

Crimson the road that Freedom treads,

We're rearing a fane of bones.

And bare feet

Weave their beat

Down the red reeking street.

Hell holds sway.

Slay! Slay!

Hate goes bellowing through the land,

Crimson-hued is my gleaming brand.

Kill! Kill! And my lips a-thrill

With hot kisses snatched in the frenzied whirl—

Raped from the lips of a noble girl.

And her brother's blood on my hand.

Rage, lust, passion-hot.

Prance, dance, you sans culotte.

This is your hour, the height of your power,

Culture, decency forgot.

 Blood! Blood! The red gleams preen

On yon fair maid the guillotine!

Vive, vive la guillotine!

Hate and slaughter, that is all;

Blood to shed and heads to fall.

Love is lust and good is lies,

Satan rides the eery skies.

Dance and sway

Whirl away

Meet and kiss, it is bliss

But to slay!

All the world's a gore-rimmed sea, lo, the devil laughs
with glee.

Come and dance then, you with me, come and caper
wild and free.

With red blood those fires are lit,

Hades' smoke is tinged with it.

And the very skies that soar

Are encrimsoned as with gore—

Yon was once a baron's head,

Now it decks a pike instead.

I salute ye, with my sword.

Here's to you, m'sieu le lord.

Much you had of wondrous wine,

Ermine coats and horses fine,

Luscious lips of dainty girls,

Snowy bosoms, gold and pearls,

None so haughty as your sneer—

Now you ride a common's spear.

Here's to you! In hell you burn.

I am on the upward turn
Of the slow revolving Wheel
With my reign of blood and steel.
O'er my prostrate head ye strode;
On my shoulder bent ye rode.
You the whip-man, I the clown
Till I rose to tread you down.
They will rise to trample me—
For the moment I am free.
Through the ribs the winds may drone
Now the world is all mine own.
Mine to lust, to rage, to dance!
Vive la Freedom! Vive la France!

The Tempter

Something tapped me on the shoulder
Something whispered, "Come with me,
"Leave the world of men behind you,
"Come where care may never find you
"Come and follow, let me bind you
"Where, in that dark, silent sea,
"Tempest of the world ne'er rages;
"There to dream away the ages,
"Heedless of Time's turning pages,

"Only, come with me."

"Who are you?" I asked the phantom,
"I am rest from Hate and Pride.
"I am friend to king and beggar,
"I am Alpha and Omega,
"I was councilor to Hagar
"But men call me suicide."
I was weary of tide breasting,
Weary of the world's behesting,
And I lusted for the resting
As a lover for his bride.

And my soul tugged at its moorings
And it whispered, "Set me free.
"I am weary of this battle,
"Of this world of human cattle,
"All this dreary noise and prattle.
"This you owe to me."
Long I sat and long I pondered,
On the life that I had squandered,
O'er the paths that I had wandered
Never free.

In the shadow panorama
Passed life's struggles and its fray.

And my soul tugged with new vigor,
Huger grew the phantom's figure,
As I slowly tugged the trigger,
Saw the world fade swift away.
Through the fogs old Time came striding,
Radiant clouds were 'bout me riding,
As my soul went gliding, gliding,
From the shadow into day.

Tides

I am weary of birth and battle,
    Seasons and Time and tide,
Of the ocean's empty rattle.
    And the woman at my side.

I am weary of pain and revel,
    And eyes that glitter or weep;
I will sell my soul to the Devil
    For a thousand years of sleep.

Then never a dream shall haunt me,
    And never a star shall rise,
Nor a shadow come to daunt me
    In the blackness over my eyes.

There shall be no name or number
    Of the seasons over me;
I shall know the tides of slumber
    As a sunken ship, the sea.

And when I shall wake hereafter,
    And the Devil comes for his gain,
I will crush him with crimson laughter
    And turn to my sleep again.

To a Woman

Though fathoms deep you sink me in the mould,
Locked in with thick-lapped lead and bolted wood,
Yet rest not easy in your lover's arms;
Let him beware to stand where I have stood.

I shall not fail to burst my ebon case,
And thrust aside the clods with fingers red:
Your blood shall turn to ice to see my face
Look from the shadows on your midnight bed.

To face the dead, he, too, shall wake in vain,
My fingers at his throat, your scream his knell;

He will not see me tear you from your bed,
And drag you by your golden hair to Hell.

To the Contended

Bide by the fluted iron walls
   Take ye a serving wench to wife;
Drown in the pot the bugle's calls,
   Trade your spear for a peddler's knife.
   Turn to the vendor's paltry strife,
     Gird ye round with doors and bars
Safely snore in the lap of Life—
   I must follow the restless stars.

Wait at the doors of your master's halls
   —For the faithful server, boards are rife—
Make no oath when the whip-lash falls—
   Hark to the counsel of your wife;
   Trade your harp for a peddler's fife.
     But gods, the spray and the plunging spars!
Here is my heart—in the heart of Life
   And I must follow the restless stars

     Envoi
King, there are stallions in golden stalls,

106

But bars of sapphire are only bars!
Bide in peace in the high safe halls—
   I must follow the restless stars.

Toper

Toil, cares, annoyances all fade away;
   I care not who may run for President.
I drowse and swing my rum the live-long day,
And watch the shallops skimming o'er the bay.

A Tribute to the Sportsmanship of the Fans

Headlock, hammerlock, toss him on his bean again,
   Jump on his belly and boot him in the hips,
Clamp the scissors on his neck
      and choke him till he's green again
      Get the fans wild-eyed, with froth on their lips.

Barlock, body-slam, nibble on his ears again—
   Its just like eating cabbage—and kick him in the
groin,
Butt him in the belly, that brings the cheers again,
   The fans want a run for their hard-spent coin.

Flying-mare, toe-hold, twist his neck around again,
  Wrap his legs around his waist and tie them in a
knot,
Stamp in his mouth so his teeth cannot be found
again,
  The fans paid their money so make it good and hot.

Stranglehold, leg-split, jerk his knee-caps loose again,
  Crack his ribs and break his arms, leave him life-
long lame,
Send him out on a shutter—then listen to the boos
again,
  The kind fans howling that the battle was too tame.

Visions

I cannot believe in a paradise
Glorious, undefiled,
For gates all scrolled and streets of gold
Are tales for a dreaming child.

I am too lost for shame
That it moves me unto mirth,

By Robert E. Howard

But I can vision a Hell of flame
For I have lived on earth.

The Voices Waken Memory

The blind black shadows reach inhuman arms
To draw me into darkness once again;
The brooding night wind hints of nameless harms,
And down the shadowed hill a vague refrain
Bears half-remembered ghosts to haunt my soul,
Like far-off neighing of the nightmare's foal.

But let me fix my phantom-shadowed eyes
Hard on the stars — pale points of silver light—
Here is the borderlad — here reason lies—
There, vision, gryphons, Nothing, and the Night.
Down, down, red spectres, down, and rack me not!
Out, wolves of Hell! Oh God, my pulses thrum;
The night grows fierce and blind and red and hot,
And nearer still a frim insistent drum.

I will not look into the shadows — No!
The star shall grip and hold my frantic gaze—
But even in the stars black visions grow,
And dragons writhe with iron eyes ablaze.

Oh Gods that raised my blindness with your curse,
And let me see the horrid shapes behind
All outward veils that cloak the universe,
The loathsome demon-spells that bind and blind,
Since even the stars are noisome, foul and fell,
Let me glut deep with memory dreams of hell.

The Weakling

I died in sin and forthwith went to Hell;
I made myself at home upon the coals
Where seas of flame break on the cinder shoals.
Till Satan came and said with angry yell,
"You there—divulge what route by which you fell."
"I spent my youth among the flowing bowls,
"Wasted my life with women of dark souls,
"Died brothel-fighting—drunk on muscatel."

Said he, "My friend, you've been directed wrong:
"You've naught to recommend you for our feasts—
"Like factory owners, brokers, elders, priests;
"The air for you! This place is for the strong!"
Then as I pondered, minded to rebel,
He laughed and forthwith kicked me out of Hell.

By Robert E. Howard

A sappe ther wos and that a crumbe manne...

A sappe ther wos and that a crumbe manne
Whoe from the timee that he firs beganne
To jazzen oute he lopved rapery,
And many a damsel sat himme on his knee.
As far as goeth manne he had wente,
And many a virgin's gude name hadde bente.
Betimes among the dames of seventeen,
And jazzen all the nighte at Racine.
To Philadelphia hadde been alsoe
Ageyne another trull in Chicagoe.
And many a damsel hadde proved fickle,
"Gude sirs," quote, "A maiden for an ickle
"Her pantys taken down for any manne,
"I hode you sirs, ageyne the whole damn clanne."
And forthwith bought a ticket to New Yorke
Because Hisse wife expected ther the storke.

After the trumps are sounded...

After the trumps are sounded
　　Over the fading world
After the drums are silent
　　And the lastmost flag is furled,

111

May we enjoy what we long for
   A boon that we sinners may tell
The most that we have to hope for
   A comfortable berth in Hell.

Against the blood red moon a tower stands...

Against the blood red moon a tower stands;
   An everlasting silence haunts the place.
It was not reared by any human hands,
   The silent symbol of a shadowy race.
There, long ago, I stole through ancient night
   My footsteps woke strange echoes through the hour;
Strange specters walked with me through mazy light.
   I left my soul, a ghost to haunt the tower.

All the crowd...

All the crowd
Meek and proud
Yellin' loud
"Knock him out!"
Queer,
How clear

By Robert E. Howard

I hear
Every shout.
Sure, show!
Let 'em know
Every blow
Every clout.
First a left,
All my heft,
His guard's reft,
Great fun.
Then a right,
Full might.
My fight.
I've won.

And Dempsey climbed into the ring and the crowd...

"And Dempsey climbed into the ring and the crowd sneered.
And Carl Morris climbed into the ring and the crowd yelled,
"Sock his damned jaw!"
And Dempsey hit Carl, by Hell!

And Carl hit the floor, by Hell!
And the crowd yelled, "You're the boy Jack!"

Hills of the North! Lavender hills...

Hills of the North! Lavender hills.
Blue hills, tipped with crystal
Defying the ages.
Hills, high peaks where eagles wheel,
Where wild winds shout forever,
Whirling the snow
Like a mad dervish.

Match a toad with a far-winged hawk...

Match a toad with a far-winged hawk,
A scarlet rose with a thistle stalk;
A stagnant pond with the white sea-tide—
You match the friendship of Bob and Clyde.
Clyde was a plucker of gems divine—
Bob was half a poet, half devil-swine.
One of them mounted the gods' own peak,
Out of the world's vile muck and reek,
Up from the world-path's ruck and slime,

Climbed on a ladder of godlike rhyme.—
One of them made his bid for fame,
Scorched his wing at the Muses' flame,
Warped his soul like a brooding devil
Found at last, and kept to, his level.
A friendship strange—yet it lasted on
Till their lives had faded to dusk from dawn.
Friendship of a falcon for a mugger—
Gods' own poet and third-rate slugger.
Lived their lives, friend unto friend—
Each in his own way met his end.
One of them passed like a Median king—
One of them died in a boxing ring.
One of them passed on a distant shore
Where the breakers answered the sea-wind's roar.
High on the crags he stood at bay,
Laughed like a god o'er the din of the fray;
Crimson the cliffs and red his sword,
One man facing a blood-crazed horde;
Man after man fell to his blade,
Laughed as he faced them, unafraid.
They swarmed like demons; what did he care?
Beauty and glory and pride were there;
Crag and mountain, ocean and sky,
Glorying to see a strong man die.
Laughed on the crags like a white limbed god,

For he knew the ways that the godlings trod—
He had scaled all peaks of glory. Last
With a snatch of song on his lips he passed.
One heard the tumult of throngs outbreak
As he writhed on the matt like a wounded snake,
Striving to get his legs beneath—
Red oaths ebbed through his broken teeth—
Above him the ring-light's garishblaze,
Sordid faces leered through the haze,
Foreign voices venting foul spleen,
Scents of unwashed forms obscene—
Shouts that flickered the ring-light's shine
"Stand up and fight, you yellow swine!"
Then the darkness loomed like a mighty tide
And he gasped out a crimson curse and died.
Thus they lived their lives friend unto friend,
And each in his own way met his end.
Match a toad with a far-winged hawk,
A crimson rose with a thistle stalk;
A stagnant pond with the ocean's tide—
You match the friendship of Bob and Clyde.
Friend unto friend, they lived their days,
Friend unto friend they walked their ways.

By Robert E. Howard

Mingle my dust with the burning brand...

Mingle my dust with the burning brand,
  Scatter it free to the sky
Fling it wide on the ocean's sand,
  From peaks where the vultures fly.

Let it drift with the drifting tide,
  And flit o'er the artic floe,
Let it spin and ride where the snow-storms hide
  And the wild ice-field winds blow.

Let it mingle with desert sand,
  And the waves of a tropic sea,
When the roaring surge sweeps o'er the strand
  And the ocean winds shout free.

Moonlight and shadows barred the land...

Moonlight and shadows barred the land;
Night breathed like some great living thing.
The Seeker rested chin in hand
And heard the night wind's whispering.
He heard like songs of vanished men
The waving branches answer then.

"Lords of the seas of silence, old as the word of God,
We are the ancient people, haters of chain and rod."

Old Faro Bill was a man of might...

Old Faro Bill was a man of might
  In the days when the West was young,
He drank a gallon of booze each night—
  The toughest galoot unhung!
Oh, some men shrink at the sight of blood!
  Bill roomed in a cougar's lair
And for tobacco he carried a cud
  Of Mexican prickly pear!
Old Faro came of a wolfish breed,
  When he was a suckling child
He laughed at the marahuana weed
  For he said that is was too mild.
Old Faro he was a buffalo
  When it came to rough-and-tumble,
He laid the toughest battlers low
  With never a miss or fumble.
Some men stammer and halt and pause
  At the sight of lover's moons,
But Faro married a hundred squaws
  And a couple of octaroons.

By Robert E. Howard

Rebel souls from the falling dark...

Rebel souls from the falling dark,
  What are the crowns you gain?
The quenching night of a dungeon stark
  And the brine of the rusty chain.
The taunt and the tang of the bitter blood,
  And the grim of the grisly bars,
The friar's chant and the hangman's hood—
  And a star amid the stars!

Scarlet and gold are the stars tonight...

Scarlet and gold are the stars tonight,
  The river runs silver below the bridge—
But the hour shall come when the dawn grows white
  Over the eastern ridge.

Your face is a dim white flower of night,
  In your arms unheeded the hours fall—
But the dawn makes hearts grow strange and light,
  And the far lands call.

Swords glimmered up the pass...

Swords glimmered up the pass
Fringing the grim dark mass.
There was blood on the grass;
Red blood
But the flood
Far below lumbered on to the east and the dawn—
When all men are gone.
Shall not they,
Hill and stream,
As today
Gleam and dream,
Forgetting forever in majesty still
That men climbed the hill or died on the river.
High on the great black crags
Like hags
Brooding for death and slaughter,
We waited
With the thirst of our blades unsated
And below us rippled the water.
We two—you and I
Last to die.
At bay there we stood and the wind in our hair
Shook the iron clawed brood of the black eagle's lair.
They came in the flame of the thundering dawn

By Robert E. Howard

Driven and drawn
By the spate of their hate and the fate of their lust
For the glimmering dust,
They dreamed they could hold, the traitor of gold,
The breaker of thrust.
And we laughed in the bend of a curse that our
blades, they
were virgin of rust
Then from his bed
The great sun clambered red;
His gleams lit up the lances and the banners of the
foe;
The cohorts clambered sealing our doom beyond
repealing;
Behind our boulders kneeling e hurled out lead below.
Many a bastard there
Of that dark band
Clutched with a nerveless hand
The mocking air.
Man after man, one by one
Dropped in the eye of the sun
To the crack of the ball;
Reeled from the sombre cliff
Grim and stiff,
And the river below drank his fall.
Two men—and we laughed and we swore

In the fringer of the rifle smoke's plume,
Twomen—and we laughed at the roar
Of a whole army bringing our doom.
And our rifles stammered and yammered,
Carving the air with red laces
Till our powder was burning their faces
As up to our muzzles they clambered.
You rose,
And you jeered—
In the beard
Of our foes
You hurled gold.
And some of them clutched it with screams,
   and some in the clutching grew cold.
And you roared to the horde:
"Here's the price of Hell's thunder!"
And the leap of your sword
Rent a bosom a-sunder.
I swung up the stock
Of my empty gun
And the crash and the shock
Broke the brains out of one.
Then smoke veiled the sun
And blood, cliff and rock.
A reeking red carpet we made and we laid
With the crash of my gun and the slash of your blade.

Bullets jerked at us,
Knives stung;
Sword points dirked at us,
Gun stocks swung. Like reddened leopards we sprung.
And they forced us back to the lip of the pass
    that over the river hung.
We were blackened with powder,
Red with blood
Ever louder we heard the flood.
Your blade was a shard on a battered hilt,
Your grip slipped on the blood you'd split.
From my rifle the splintered stock was rent
And the barrel was twisted, burst and bent.
The last charge came—fierce faces rose
To go blank under our last great blows.
Flame in our faces waved its sheet
And we felt the gulf yawn under our feet...
Roaring our final oaths we fell
And crashed together into Hell.

The spiders of weariness come on me...

The spiders of weariness come on me
To weave wide webs on my brain.

I must go to the night and the sighing sea
And the drive of the drifting rain.

There were three lads who went their destined ways...

There were three lads who went their destined ways
  Bewildered by this thing that men call Life
Toiled through the week and idled leisure days.
  And cursed the world but knew the world was rife
With thing of beauty. Even they could see.
  They reveled in old tales of ages hoary
  And plagued by souls vague reaching out for glory,
But knew dim, uncertain longing to be free.

They saw, they felt but could not put in words
  The things of beauty that oft met their eyes,
Waving of blossoms and the flight of birds,
  The tints of sun-set fading from the skies.
    They dimly glimpsed the sky-kissed mountain
crest
    And felt chargrin of failure, dim unrest.

Blasphemous, showing their deep joy at verses,
Praising an artist with deep, sulphurous curses.

When their souls thrilled they knew but naught to swear
   Admiring cursed at lakes by breezes kissed,
"Say, look at that damned elm waving there."
   And vaunt its praise with oaths that fairly hissed.
They named, if chose, a demi-god a lout
   Sneered at the thought that man-kind was their brother
Yet they could see a pretty girl without
   Licking their lips and elbowing each other.
And they could see young saplings in the shade
   And think of dancing girls. Could see
The sapling's litheness in a tender maid.
   Could revel in the winds that whisper free.

"Say, boy, you see that moon just coming up,
   Throwing its banners like long, silver teeth,
Say, I can think that it's some sea-king's golden cup—
   Look there, white clouds above and purple hills beneath.
You know old pard, I guess that I'm a fool.
   But I have got a lot of thoughts in me—
But what's the use? There never was a school
   Could teach a fellow to write poetry.
And yet it's in my soul. I'd like to tell
   The things I feel and see and sometimes think

Yet I can't catch and put them into ink—
My thoughts are great—my speech so barren. Hell!"

And in impotent anger, kick the sand
And gesture vaguely with a toil-worn hand.

And sometimes they would put on leather gloves
    And therewith deal each other manful blows,
    Pausing perchance to shake a bleeding nose,
    Admire a leafy bough or budding rose,
Through loosened teeth quote poets songs of loves.
They took delights in rough and savage games,
Strong drink, and called each other scorching names.
Yet they would turn aside to small a flower.
Oftentimes
Would sit them down and seek to make some rhymes.

Then feeling their dim soul-glories wane, morosely go
To see a prize-fight or a picture show.

There's an isle far away on the breast of the sea...

There's an isle far away on the breast of the sea,
A gem that is set in the stars of the bay,
And it lives in the hearts of the wanderers who stray,

(And begob it's too good for such spalpeens as ye!)

Oh the sorrow on them that have sailed from its
swards!
On the thoughts that they think and the sighs that
they sigh!
Is it liquor alone that is dimming their eye?
(With the graft that they get from misvotin' the
wards.)

Oh, oft to that isle the fond memory flies!
To the brooks where they sported, so young and so
chaste
And the dear drowsy shores that they left in such haste
(For the stealin' of cows and the tellin' of lies.)

There the soft fleecy clouds on the mountains repose,
And the breeze is a kiss and perfume to the mind,
And love reigns supreme and peace sits enshrined.
(So shut your damned mouth or I'll break your
damned nose.)

Oh the men of the isle are all loyal and bold
And the women are lovely and fair to the eye;
Ochone for the ones who left with a sigh.
(Betrayin' their friends for the Englishman's gold.)

Oh never the love of that island shall slack
As long as her sons shall roam the world round,
For a country so beautiful will ne'er be found.
(God pity the bastards that have to go back.)

We are the duckers of crosses...

We are the duckers of crosses,
   We are the swingers of swings.
We count our gains and our losses
   In all of the fourth rate rings.
We are the bums and the slackers
   Swiggers of Ancient Crow.
Yet the fans pay sixteen smackers
   To see us knocked for a row.
Bout losers and bout forsakers
   They hand us a-many slams,
For we are the set-ups and fakers,
   We are the fourth-rate hams!
We are the takers of slams and blips!
   Jester and ring-side clown!
But sometimes we go with our trunks on our hips
   And jerk us a title down!
Taking bout that champs are shying,

By Robert E. Howard

Where the ring gong clangs and thrums
Where the swining mitts are flying—
 We are the fourth-rate bums!